PIANO · VOCAL · GUITAR

THE BIG BOOK OF MOVIE MUSIC

ISBN 0-7935-1627-7

HAL•LEONARD®
CORPORATION
7777 W. BLUEMOUND RD. P.O. BOX 13819 MILWAUKEE, WI 53213

Visit Hal Leonard Online at
www.halleonard.com

CONT

ALL FOR LOVE

from Walt Disney Pictures' THE THREE MUSKETEERS

Words and Music by BRYAN ADAMS,
ROBERT JOHN "MUTT" LANGE and MICHAEL KAMEN

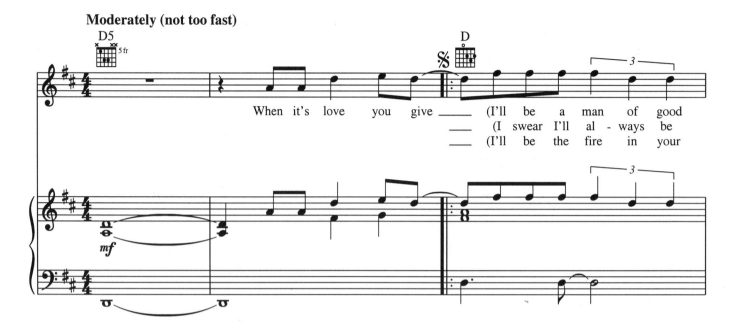

AMERICA
from the Motion Picture THE JAZZ SINGER

Words and Music by
NEIL DIAMOND

Moderately bright

F

mf

Far,

we've been trav - el - ing far,

with - out __ a   home, __

but not with - out a   star. __

Got a dream to take __ them there. They're com - ing to A -

mer - i - ca. Got a dream, __ they've come __ to share.

They're com - ing to A - mer - i - ca. They're com - ing to A -

mer - i - ca. They're com - ing to A - mer - i - ca.

BACK TO THE FUTURE
from the Universal Motion Picture BACK TO THE FUTURE

By ALAN SILVESTRI

MCA Music Publishing

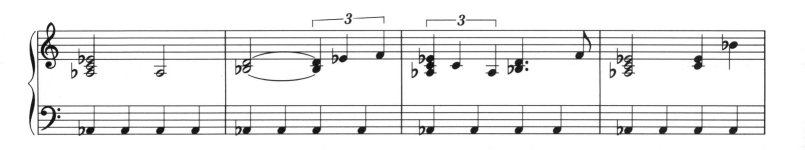

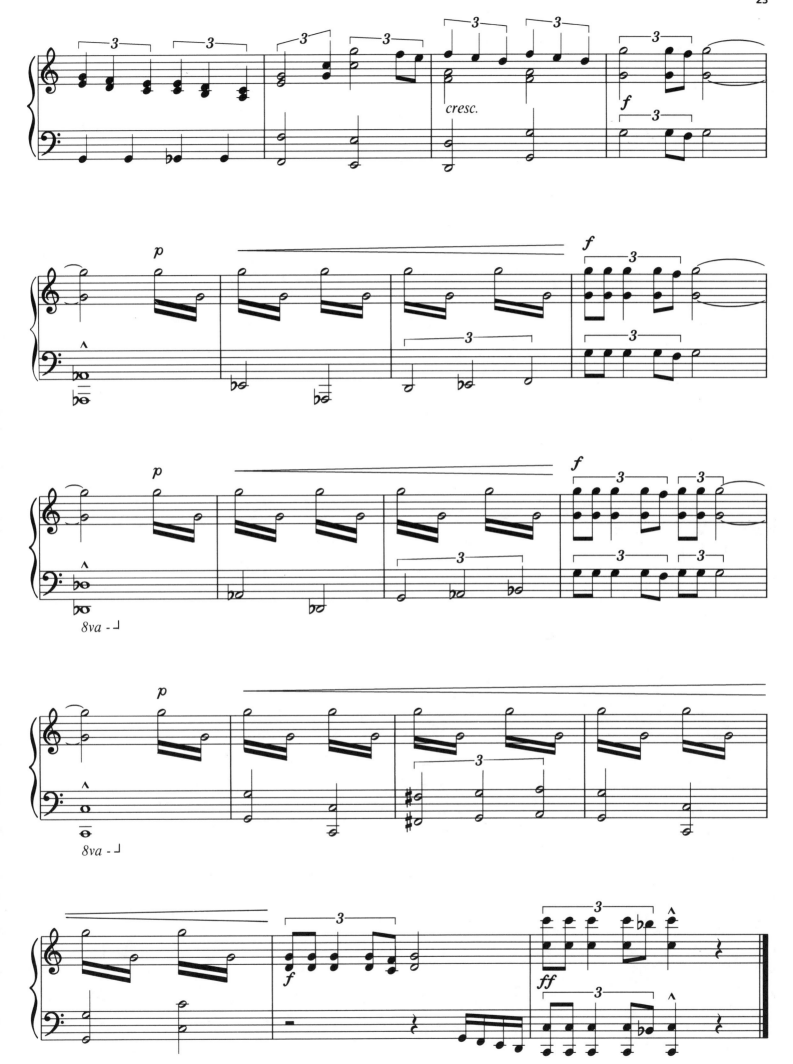

BEAUTY AND THE BEAST
from Walt Disney's BEAUTY AND THE BEAST

Lyrics by HOWARD ASHMAN
Music by ALAN MENKEN

CANDLE ON THE WATER

from Walt Disney's PETE'S DRAGON

Words and Music by AL KASHA
and JOEL HIRSCHHORN

I'll be your can-dle on the wa-ter, my love for you will al-ways
I'll be your can-dle on the wa-ter 'til ev-'ry wave is warm and

burn. I know you're lost and drift-ing, but the clouds are lift-ing.
bright. My soul is there be-side you, let this can-dle guide you;

Don't give up; you have some-where to turn.
soon you'll see a gold-en stream of light.

BLAZE OF GLORY
featured in the film YOUNG GUNS II

Words and Music by
JON BON JOVI

wake up   in   the   morn - ing   and I   raise my wear-y   head,_____   I've got an

night   I   go to bed,   I pray the   Lord my   soul   to keep._   No   I ain't

no-one's   son.   Call   me   young _   gun.
de-vil's   son.   Call   me   young _

You

gun.

Guitar solo ad lib.

Play 3 times

Additional Lyrics (Album version)

2. When you're brought into this world
   They say you're born in sin.
   Well, at least they gave me something
   I didn't have to steal or have to win.
   Well, they tell me that I'm wanted
   Yeah, I'm a wanted man.
   I'm a colt in your stable,
   I'm what Cain was to Abel.
   Mister, catch me if you can.

CHANGE THE WORLD

featured on the Motion Picture Soundtrack PHENOMENON

Words and Music by GORDON KENNEDY,
TOMMY SIMS and WAYNE KIRKPATRICK

CINEMA PARADISO

from CINEMA PARADISO

Music by
ENNIO MORRICONE

Simply, with feeling

COLE'S SONG

from MR. HOLLAND'S OPUS

Words by JULIAN LENNON and JUSTIN CLAYTON
Music by MICHAEL KAMEN

COLORS OF THE WIND
from Walt Disney's POCAHONTAS

Music by ALAN MENKEN
Lyrics by STEPHEN SCHWARTZ

You

think I'm an ig-no-rant sav-age, and you've been so man-y plac-es, I guess it must be so. But

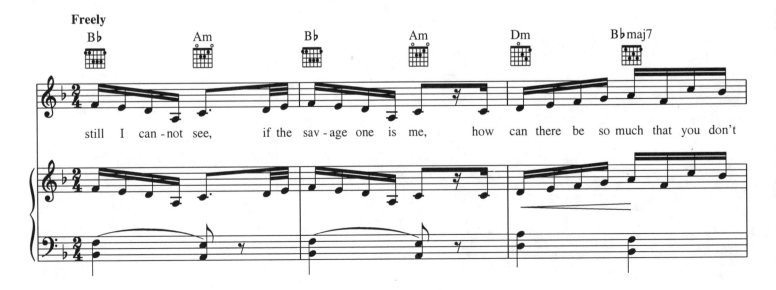

still I can-not see, if the sav-age one is me, how can there be so much that you don't

THE ENGLISH PATIENT

from THE ENGLISH PATIENT

Written by
GABRIEL YARED

DO YOU KNOW WHERE YOU'RE GOING TO?

Theme from MAHOGANY

Words by GERRY GOFFIN
Music by MIKE MASSER

DRIVING MISS DAISY
from DRIVING MISS DAISY

By HANS ZIMMER

ENDLESS LOVE

from ENDLESS LOVE

Words and Music by
LIONEL RICHIE

Moderately slow

My love, ___ there's on - ly you in my life, ___
Two hearts, ___ two hearts that beat as ___ one; ___

the on - ly thing that's right. ___ My
our lives have just be - gun. ___ For -

first ___ love, ___ you're ev - 'ry breath that I take, ___
ev - er, ___ I'll hold you close in my arms, ___

Oh, _____ and __ love, _____

THEME FROM E.T.
(The Extra-Terrestrial)
from the Universal Picture E.T. (THE EXTRA-TERRESTRIAL)

Music by JOHN WILLIAMS

Piano Solo

MCA Music Publishing

EXHALE
(Shoop Shoop)
from the Original Soundtrack Album WAITING TO EXHALE

Words and Music by
BABYFACE

Easy R&B ballad

F(add9)

C/E

1. Ev - 'ry - one falls in love some - times. _____ Some-times it's
2.,3. laugh, some-times you'll cry. _____ Life nev - er

Dm7

C

wrong _____ and some - times it's right. For ev - 'ry
tells _ us _____ the whens or whys. When you've got

F(add9)

C/E

win some - one must fail, but there comes a
friends to wish you well, you'll find a

THE EXODUS SONG
from EXODUS

Words by PAT BOONE
Music by ERNEST GOLD

EYE OF THE TIGER
Theme from ROCKY III

Words and Music by FRANK SULLIVAN
and JIM PETERIK

FLASHDANCE...WHAT A FEELING

from the Paramount Picture FLASHDANCE

Lyrics by KEITH FORSEY and IRENE CARA
Music by GIORGIO MORODER

FOR ALL WE KNOW
from the Motion Picture LOVERS AND OTHER STRANGERS

Words by ROBB WILSON and JAMES GRIFFIN
Music by FRED KARLIN

GODZILLA - MAIN THEME (OPENING TITLES)

from the TriStar Motion Picture GODZILLA

Written and Composed by
DAVID ARNOLD

Mysteriously, steadily

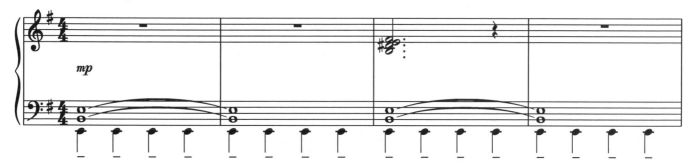

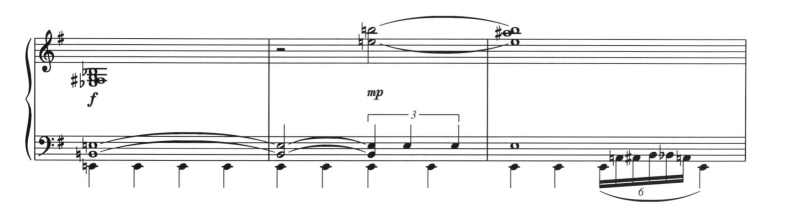

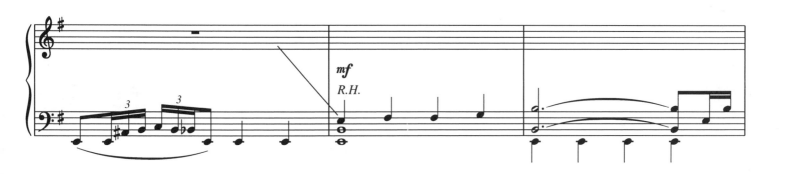

FOR THE FIRST TIME

from ONE FINE DAY

Words and Music by ALLAN RICH,
JAMES NEWTON HOWARD and JUD FRIEDMAN

GIGI
from GIGI

Words by ALAN JAY LERNER
Music by FREDERICK LOEWE

GO THE DISTANCE
from Walt Disney Pictures' HERCULES

Music by ALAN MENKEN
Lyrics by DAVID ZIPPEL

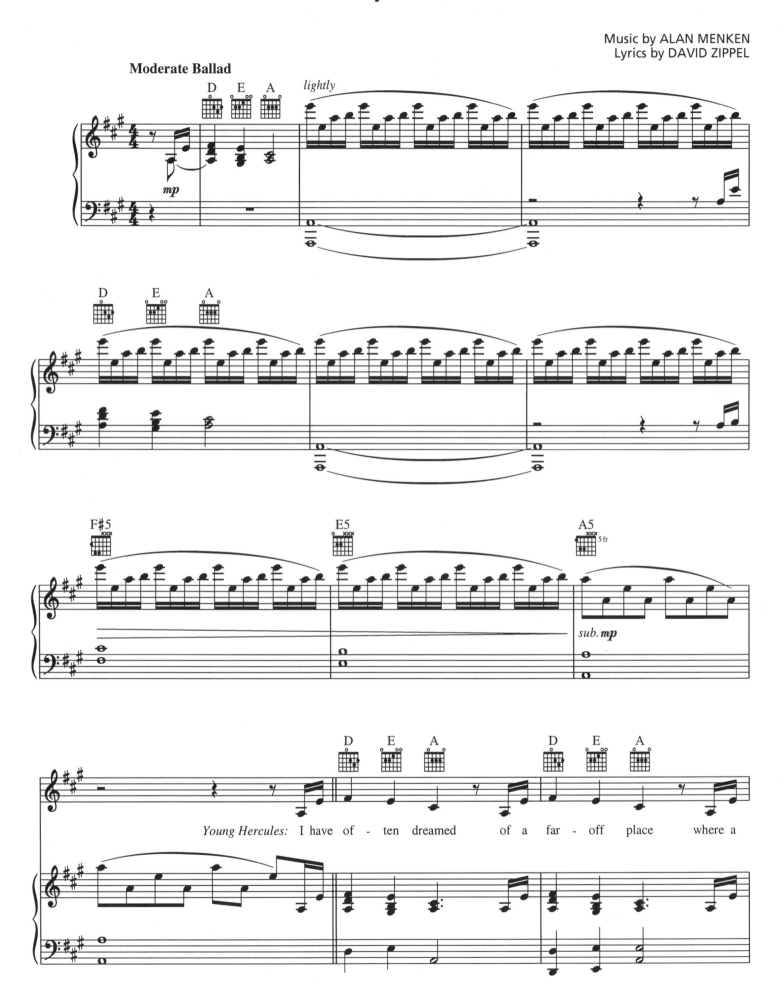

Young Hercules: I have of-ten dreamed of a far-off place where a

114

A HARD DAY'S NIGHT
from A HARD DAY'S NIGHT

Words and Music by JOHN LENNON
and PAUL McCARTNEY

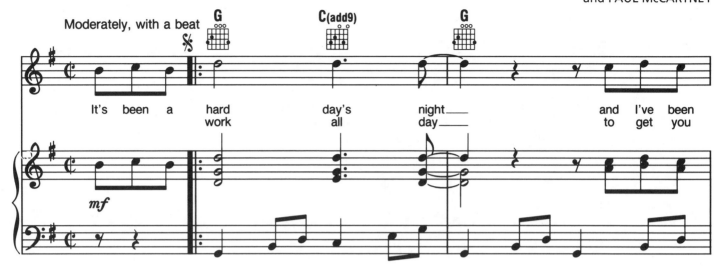

It's been a hard day's night _____ and I've been
Moderately, with a beat
It's been a hard work all day _____ to get you

work-ing like a dog. _____ It's been a hard day's night
mon-ey to buy you things. _____ And it's worth it just to hear you say _____

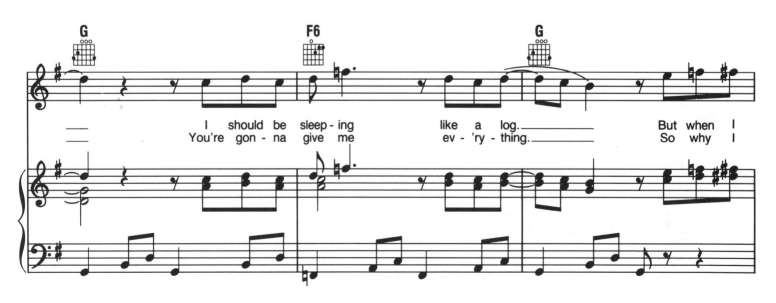

_____ I should be sleep-ing like a log. But when I
_____ You're gon-na give me ev-'ry-thing. So why I

HUSH HUSH, SWEET CHARLOTTE

from HUSH HUSH, SWEET CHARLOTTE

Words and Music by MACK DAVID
and FRANK DeVOL

Slowly and sweetly

Hush, hush, sweet Char - lotte, Char-lotte, don't you cry; Hush, hush sweet Char - lotte, I'll love you till I die. Oh,

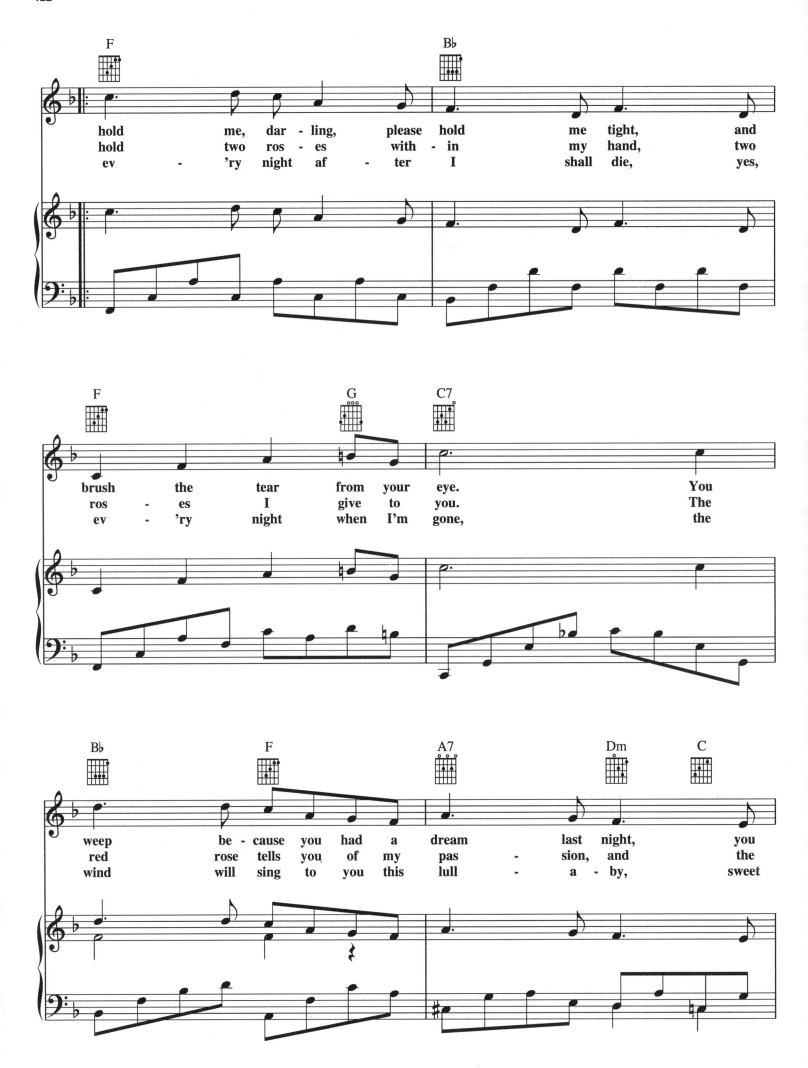

HOPELESSLY DEVOTED TO YOU
from GREASE

Words and Music by
JOHN FARRAR

I FINALLY FOUND SOMEONE

from THE MIRROR HAS TWO FACES

Words and Music by BARBRA STREISAND, MARVIN HAMLISCH,
R. J. LANGE and BRYAN ADAMS

I SAY A LITTLE PRAYER

featured in the TriStar Motion Picture MY BEST FRIEND'S WEDDING

Lyric by HAL DAVID
Music by BURT BACHARACH

Moderately fast

(1.) The mo - ment I wake up,
(2.) I run ___ for the bus, dear.
(D.S.) *Instrumental solo*

be - fore ___ I put on my make - up,
While rid - ing, I think of us, dear.

I I (I

I WILL FOLLOW HIM

(I Will Follow You)

featured in the Motion Picture SISTER ACT

English Lyric by NORMAN GIMBEL and ARTHUR ALTMAN
Original Lyric by JACQUES PLANTE
Music by J.W. STOLE and DEL ROMA

I'M HANS CHRISTIAN ANDERSEN

from HANS CHRISTIAN ANDERSEN

By FRANK LOESSER

I'M STILL HERE

featured in the Motion Picture POSTCARDS FROM THE EDGE

Words and Music by
STEPHEN SONDHEIM

IF WE HOLD ON TOGETHER
from THE LAND BEFORE TIME

Words and Music by JAMES HORNER
and WILL JENNINGS

Don't lose your way with each pass-ing day.
Souls in the wind must learn how to bend,

You've come so far, don't throw it a-way.
seek out a star, hold on to the end.

Live be-liev-ing
Val-ley, moun-tain,

IT MIGHT AS WELL BE SPRING

from STATE FAIR

Lyrics by OSCAR HAMMERSTEIN II
Music by RICHARD RODGERS

The things I used to like I don't like an-y-more. I want a lot of oth-er things I've

nev-er had be-fore. It's just like moth-er says, I "sit a-round and mope" pre-

tend-ing I am won-der-ful and know-ing I'm a dope. _____ I'm as

THEME FROM "JAWS"
from the Universal Picture JAWS

By JOHN WILLIAMS

Very steady and threatening

MCA Music Publishing

JESSICA'S THEME
(Breaking in the Colt)
from THE MAN FROM SNOWY RIVER

By BRUCE ROWLAND

CODA

KING OF WISHFUL THINKING

from the Motion Picture PRETTY WOMAN

Words and Music by MARTIN PAGE,
PETER COX and RICHARD DRUMMIE

talk of the town, _____ may-be I can fool my - self. _____ } And I'll get
hole in my heart. _____ And now I've got to fool my - self. _____

o - ver you, ___ I know I will. ___ I'll pre - tend my ship's _ not

sink - ing. ___ And I'll tell my - self ___ I'm o - ver you, _ 'cause I'm the

To Coda ⊕

king of wish - ful think - ing. _____

THE JOHN DUNBAR THEME
from DANCES WITH WOLVES

By JOHN BARRY

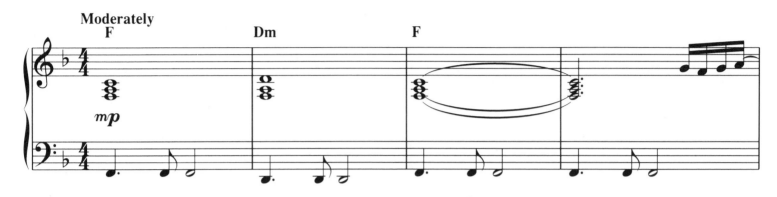

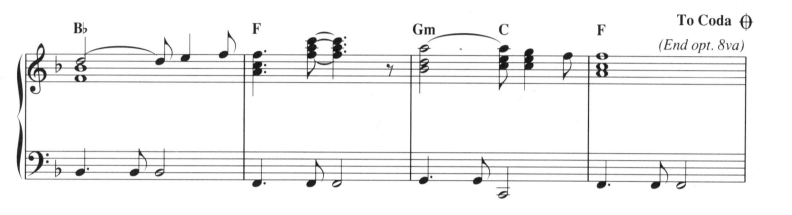

To Coda ⊕
(End opt. 8va)

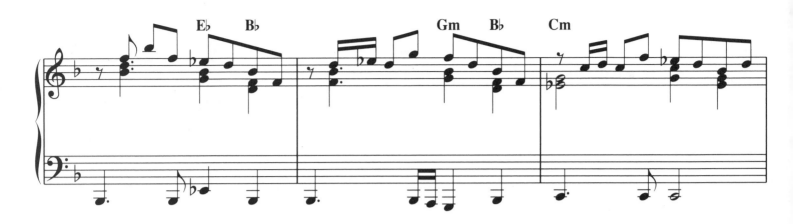

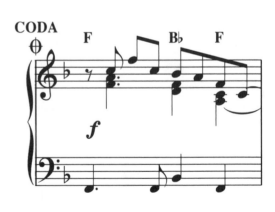

KOKOMO
from the Motion Picture COCKTAIL

Words and Music by MIKE LOVE, TERRY MELCHER,
JOHN PHILLIPS and SCOTT McKENZIE

Moderately bright

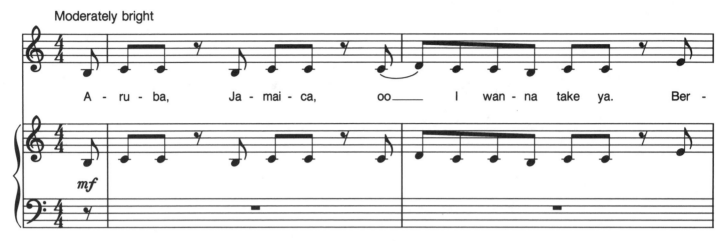

A - ru - ba, Ja - mai - ca, oo___ I wan - na take ya. Ber -

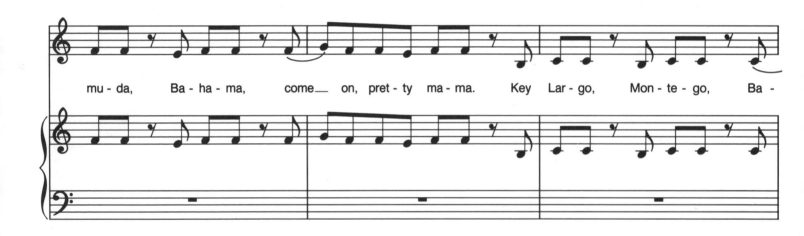

mu - da, Ba - ha - ma, come___ on, pret - ty ma - ma. Key Lar - go, Mon - te - go, Ba -

- by, why don't we go, Ja - mai - ca. Off the Flor - i - da Keys___
We'll put out to sea___

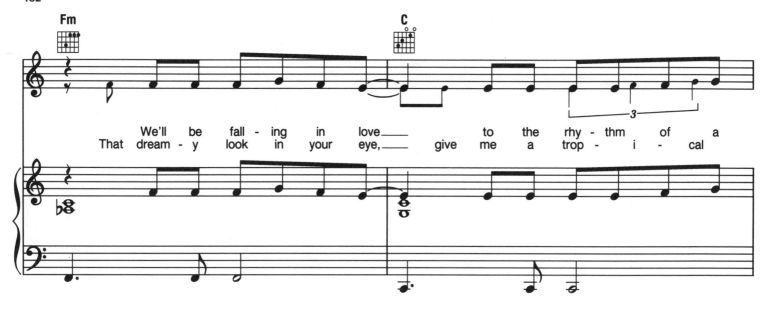

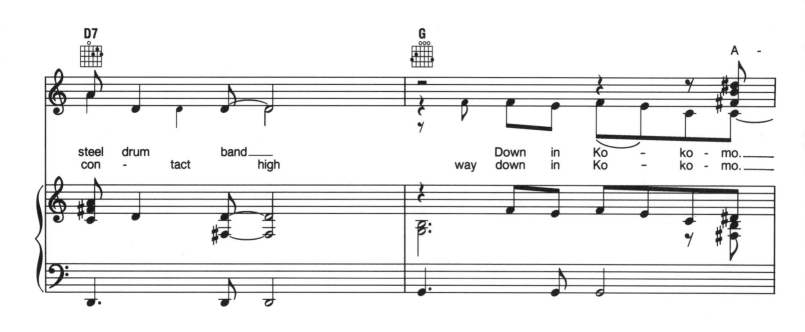

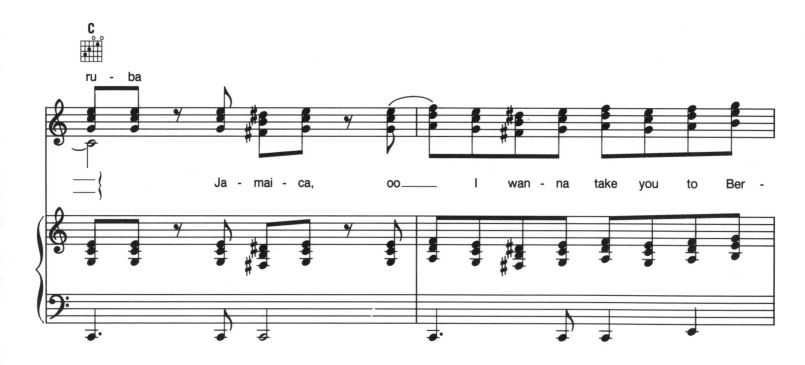

LET'S GET TOGETHER

from Walt Disney Pictures' THE PARENT TRAP

Words and Music by RICHARD M. SHERMAN
and ROBERT B. SHERMAN

LET'S HEAR IT FOR THE BOY

from the Paramount Motion Picture FOOTLOOSE

Words by DEAN PITCHFORD
Music by TOM SNOW

A MAN AND A WOMAN
(Un Homme Et Une Femme)
from A MAN AND A WOMAN

Original Words by PIERRE BAROUH
English Words by JERRY KELLER
Music by FRANCIS LAI

MCA Music Publishing

MOONLIGHT
from the Paramount Motion Picture SABRINA

Lyric by ALAN and MARILYN BERGMAN
Music by JOHN WILLIAMS

MORE
(Ti Guardero' Nel Cuore)
from the film MONDO CANE

Music by NINO OLIVIERO and RIZ ORTOLANI
Italian Lyrics by MARCELLO CIORCIOLINI
English Lyrics by NORMAN NEWELL

205

ON GOLDEN POND
Main Theme from ON GOLDEN POND

Music by DAVE GRUSIN

Very freely

p *very delicately, as though from far away*

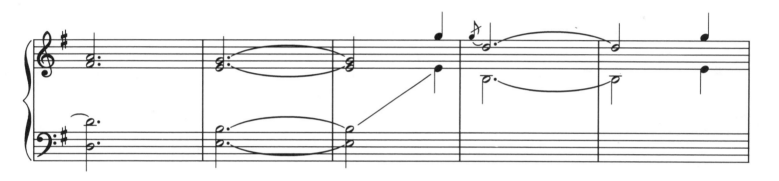

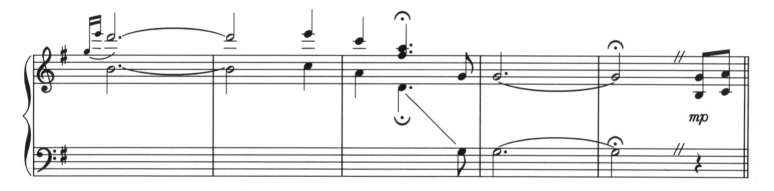

Andante rubato*

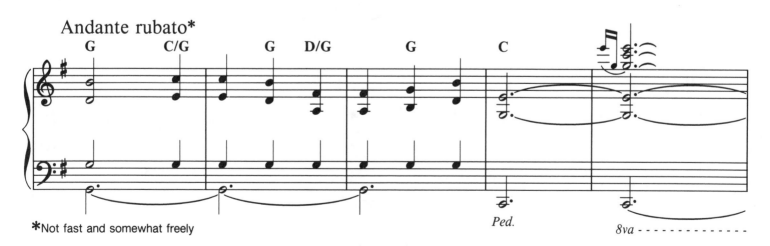

*Not fast and somewhat freely

THE MUSIC OF GOODBYE
Love Theme from OUT OF AFRICA

Music by JOHN BARRY
Words by ALAN and MARILYN BERGMAN

NEVER ON SUNDAY

from Jules Dassin's Motion Picture NEVER ON SUNDAY

Words by BILLY TOWNE
Music by MANOS HADJIDAKIS

Moderato

Refrain

Oh, you can kiss me on a Mon-day, a Mon-day, a
cool day, a hot day, a

Mon-day is ver-y, ver-y good. Or you can kiss me on a Tues-day, a Tues-day, a Tues-day, in fact I wish you
wet day, which-ev-er one you choose. Or try to kiss me on a gray day, a May day, a pay day, and see if I re-

would. Or you can kiss me on a Wednes-day, a Thurs-day, a Fri - day and Sat-ur-day is best.
fuse. And if you make it on a bleak day, a freak day, a week - day, why you can be my guest.

QUE SERA, SERA
(Whatever Will Be, Will Be)
from THE MAN WHO KNEW TOO MUCH

Words and Music by
JAY LIVINGSTON
and RAY EVANS

THE RAINBOW CONNECTION
from THE MUPPET MOVIE

By PAUL WILLIAMS
and KENNETH L. ASCHER

Why are there so man-y songs a-bout rain-bows, and
Who said that ev-'ry wish would be heard and an-swered when

what's on the oth-er side? _____
wished on the morn-ing star? _____

Rain-bows are vi-sions,_ but on-ly il-lu-sions, and
Some-bod-y thought of that, and some-one be-lieved it;

SOMEWHERE OUT THERE
from AN AMERICAN TAIL

Words and Music by JAMES HORNER,
BARRY MANN and CYNTHIA WEIL

MCA Music Publishing

REMEMBER ME THIS WAY

from the Universal Motion Picture CASPER

Music by DAVID FOSTER
Lyrics by LINDA THOMPSON

SEPARATE LIVES
Love Theme from WHITE NIGHTS

Words and Music by
STEPHEN BISHOP

SOMEDAY

from Walt Disney's THE HUNCHBACK OF NOTRE DAME

Music by ALAN MENKEN
Lyrics by STEPHEN SCHWARTZ

SOMEWHERE IN TIME

from SOMEWHERE IN TIME

By JOHN BARRY

Moderately slow

SOONER OR LATER
(I Always Get My Man)
from the Film DICK TRACY

Words and Music by
STEPHEN SONDHEIM

THEME FROM "SOPHIE'S CHOICE"

from SOPHIE'S CHOICE

By MARVIN HAMLISCH

R.H.

p

L.H.

8va

as though fading | *into the distance*

ppp

THEME FROM "STAR TREK® GENERATIONS"

from the Paramount Motion Picture STAR TREK GENERATIONS

Music by DENNIS McCARTHY

STAYIN' ALIVE
from SATURDAY NIGHT FEVER

Words and Music by BARRY GIBB,
MAURICE GIBB and ROBIN GIBB

TAKE MY BREATH AWAY
(Love Theme)
from the Paramount Picture TOP GUN

Words and Music by GIORGIO MORODER
and TOM WHITLOCK

THAT THING YOU DO!

from the Original Motion Picture Soundtrack THAT THING YOU DO!

Words and Music by
ADAM SCHLESINGER

THREE COINS IN THE FOUNTAIN

from THREE COINS IN THE FOUNTAIN

Words by SAMMY CAHN
Music by JULE STYNE

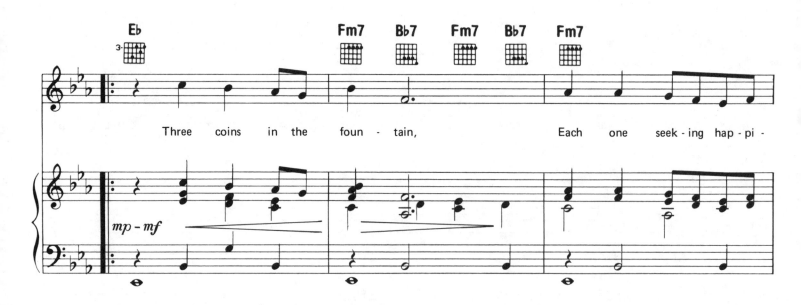

Three coins in the foun-tain, Each one seek-ing hap-pi-

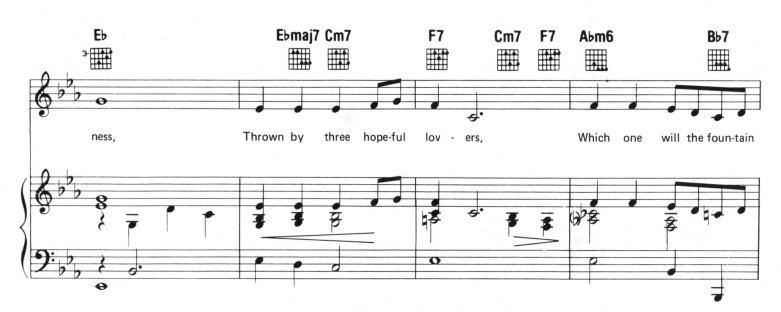

ness, Thrown by three hope-ful lov-ers, Which one will the foun-tain

UNCHAINED MELODY
featured in the Motion Picture GHOST

Lyric by HY ZARET
Music by ALEX NORTH

Moderately slow

Oh, my love, my dar - ling, I've hun - gered for your

touch a long, lone - ly time. _____

Time goes by so slow - ly and time can do so

UNDER THE SEA
from Walt Disney's THE LITTLE MERMAID

Lyrics by HOWARD ASHMAN
Music by ALAN MENKEN

UNINVITED
from the Motion Picture CITY OF ANGELS

Words and Music by
ALANIS MORISSETTE

A WINK AND A SMILE

featured in the TriStar Motion Picture SLEEPLESS IN SEATTLE

Words and Music by MARC SHAIMAN
and RAMSEY McLEAN

Moderate Swing

Lyrics:

1. I re-mem-ber the days ___ of just keep-ing time, ___ of
2. (Instrumental solo ad lib...

hang-ing a-round ___ in ___ sleep-y towns ___ for-ev-er; ___ ... end solo)

back roads emp-ty for miles. ___   Well, you
Give me a wink and a smile. ___   (continue solo...

THE WAY YOU LOOK TONIGHT

featured in the TriStar Motion Picture MY BEST FRIEND'S WEDDING

Words by DOROTHY FIELDS
Music by JEROME KERN

WHAT A WONDERFUL WORLD

featured in the Motion Picture GOOD MORNING VIETNAM

Words and Music by GEORGE DAVID WEISS
and BOB THIELE

THE WINGS OF THE DOVE
from the Miramax Motion Picture THE WINGS OF THE DOVE

By EDWARD SHEARMUR

Andante espressivo

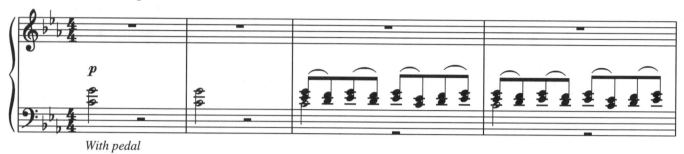

With pedal

Original key: C-sharp minor. This edition has been transposed down one half-step to be more playable.

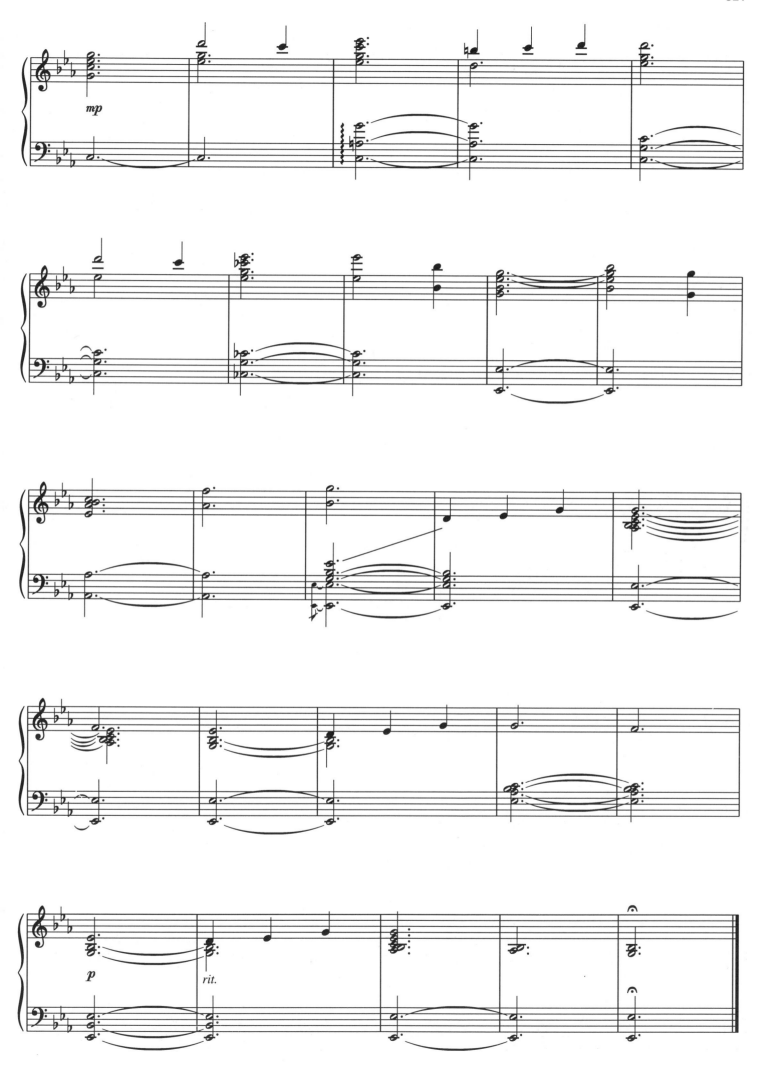

WITNESS
(Main Title)
from the Paramount Motion Picture WITNESS

Music by MAURICE JARRE

Slowly

N.C.

pp

With pedal

p

YELLOW SUBMARINE
from YELLOW SUBMARINE

Words and Music by JOHN LENNON
and PAUL McCARTNEY

YOU'VE GOT A FRIEND IN ME

from Walt Disney's TOY STORY

Music and Lyrics by
RANDY NEWMAN

You've got a friend in me.
You've got a friend in me.

You've got a friend in me.
You've got a friend in me.

When the road looks rough a-head and you're miles
You got trou-bles, then I got 'em too.

ZIP-A-DEE-DOO-DAH
from Walt Disney's SONG OF THE SOUTH

Words by RAY GILBERT
Music by ALLIE WRUBEL

Zip - a-dee doo - dah, zip - a-dee ay. ___ My, oh my, ___ what a won-der-ful day! ___ Plen - ty of sun - shine, head - in' my way. ___ Zip - a-dee doo - dah,

ZORRO'S THEME
from the TriStar Motion Picture THE MASK OF ZORRO

Written and Composed by
JAMES HORNER

Slowly, expressively